MY SMILE IS MY SUPERPOWER

GLENN STUCKI

Published by FranklinCovey Publishing, a division of FranklinCovey.

ISBN 978-1-936111-75-6

Printed in the United States of America.

PRAISE FOR MY SMILE IS MY SUPERPOWER

"Inspiring determination. Undaunted perseverance. Contagious enthusiasm. All descriptors of an incredible man named Glenn Stucki. Since Glenn was a junior-high student in my classroom, he has set goals and tenaciously pursued them until they were achieved. Glenn's personal journey paired with *The 7 Habits of Highly Effective People* is an uplifting, motivating guide that will encourage people of all abilities to lead a more successful, fulfilling, and goal-driven life."

Melanie L. Hansen,
Special Educator

"As an educator and mother of a child with special needs, it is heartwarming to see how Glenn Stucki aligns *The 7 Habits of Highly Effective People* to his abilities. This book shows it is a person's commitment to be the best they can be that makes them powerful. Taking action by using the habits can help overcome whatever challenges one faces in life and may even result in finding a superpower!"

Alicia Parsons,
Educator and Parent of a Child With Special Needs

"We often overlook the staggering statistic that one in five individuals in the U.S. has some level of disability, and each of those individuals is part of a larger family. We overlook this statistic because individuals with disabilities are invisible to the rest of us. Glenn could be one of those statistics—in his parents' basement with no path for a career, social interaction, or independence. But he beat the odds, and he did so in a way that he could share his inspirational story with others. We *see* his smile, his book, and his career and life goals. We *see* how others change how they look at disabilities when they are around Glenn. By writing this book, he gives individuals with disabilities a framework for self-improvement and hope. More importantly, Glenn gives us a tool that removes the cloak of invisibility and opens our eyes to the potential of individuals with disabilities to change the world, one person at a time."

Stephanie Mackay,
Chief Innovation Officer at the Columbus Community Center
(www.columbusserves.org)

"Recovering from a traumatic brain injury is an exceptionally difficult task for the body and the mind, as Glenn attests in this book. Some abilities may never be recovered, but the ability to choose one's response based on principles is not lost. In this book, Glenn gives a firsthand account and a road map of how to exercise that power to choose by applying habits of effectiveness. This is a hopeful message to anyone who may feel powerless."

Katherine Bailey,
Certified Pediatric Nurse Practitioner

"Glenn gives an amazing example of the power of positive thinking and attitude. It is only through the miraculous power of his thought that Glenn could have recovered and become the happy and capable person he is today."

Josh Wible,
The Friend Who Saved Glenn's Life After His Accident

All drawings and figures in this book are original works of art by Glenn Stucki and his friend Bart Hawkins.

Dedicated to Martin Luther King Jr.

TABLE OF CONTENTS

ACKNOWLEDGMENTS

I would like to thank my mom and dad for instilling in me the belief that I could overcome any obstacle that came my way, and my family for always being there for me. I'd also like to thank my aunt, Bettyanne Bruin, for arranging all of the words on all of these pages. I am so grateful for Joe Grover's help in pulling out my dream. I also appreciate Sean Covey for having enough faith in me to encourage me to write this book. I'd also like to thank Tiffany Yoast for helping me get my foundation, Ability, off the ground, for spending countless hours preparing lessons to teach with me, for going to so many board meetings, and for grants from Walmart. (Thank you, Ryan Hester, and all of the other store managers who had faith in me to donate and help my dream grow.) A special thanks also goes to my board of advisors for helping me. And lastly, thank you to all of the many wonderful people with disabilities who enable me to continually strive to be my best: I love you all!

This is my mom and dad.

FOREWORD

by Sean Covey

It is often the case that the most remarkable things in life emerge from tragedy. So it is with Glenn Stucki. At the age of 11, Glenn suffered a traumatic brain injury from a boating accident that left him in a coma for weeks. After years of rehabilitation, Glenn emerged as one of the most remarkable people you'll ever meet.

Glenn still has obvious challenges. He walks with a limp as a result of his right-side partial paralysis. His speech is slurred. At times he will pause for long periods as he struggles to put his thoughts together. It is hard for him to manage his emotions. But underneath all that is this intelligent, funny, and compassionate young man who has a knack for making everyone smile.

Since we live in the same town, it didn't take long to get to know Glenn. Everyone knows Glenn. The old lady across the street knows Glenn. The quarterback of the local university knows Glenn. The governor knows Glenn. This guy gets around! If a good party is going on, Glenn is there. If someone needs help, Glenn will pop out of nowhere to save the day. You open up the paper, and you'll read an article about Glenn. Old people love him. Young people love him. Famous people love him. Homeless people love him. When he speaks, every sentence, if written, would conclude with an exclamation point. And he always wraps up every conversation with the same line: "I love you!"

Glenn is also highly proactive. Despite his challenges, Glenn has managed to graduate from high school, get a college degree, start a nonprofit foundation, secure a steady job, and become an artist. Please take a look at the doodles and paintings that are throughout this book. These are all drawn by Glenn Stucki, who doctors said would never move his hands again.

If Glenn can't get in touch with you by phone or text, don't worry. He'll just show up at your door. A few years back, Glenn showed up at my door and said, "Sean! I just read your book on the 7 Habits for teens! I can't believe it! It is exactly me! Those are the habits I've been living all my life! We need to do something about this!"

After I helped him catch his breath, I said, "Glenn, what if you were to write a book about living the 7 Habits for people with disabilities?"

"That would be awesome!" he gushed. "When can I do it? I need to help my people!"

"What do you mean? What people?"

"People like me. People that everyone makes fun of. People who don't realize how great they are! Sean, you can help me set my people free!"

For just a moment, I pictured Moses (as played by Charlton Heston in the classic movie *The Ten Commandments*) standing before the pharaoh of Egypt and demanding that his people be set free. I had to laugh.

That is how this whole thing began. I knew that Glenn would write a good book about living well with a disability by implementing the 7 Habits, but I didn't know it would be as good as this turned out. This book is written for people with disabilities of all kinds and the families, schools, and caregivers around them. It is a story of Glenn's personal journey to success through practicing the principles of the 7 Habits, such as initiative, vision, cooperation, understanding, and renewal. It is a profound work. At its core, Glenn teaches that despite any disability we may have, we cannot afford to be victims, feel sorrow for ourselves, or be held hostage by the limitations other people place upon us. Rather, we should focus on the many things we can do, break free from the limitations placed upon us, and believe we can make a difference in the world. This is how we set ourselves free.

What makes Glenn so extraordinary is that he is fully self-aware. He realizes that his brain and body don't work like they once did. He realizes he has limitations. He is emotionally intelligent and can quickly tell if someone is patronizing him or treating him in a lesser way because of his disability. And he doesn't like it. He just wants to be treated with the same respect everyone deserves. And he wants the same for his people.

His message is simple. We are all equals. Whether we have a disability or not, no one is better or lesser than anyone else. And everyone has infinite worth and potential, or, as Glenn puts it, "Everyone has a superpower." Someone may be good at sports, another good with people, yet another good at music. For Glenn, his smile is his superpower.

PART ONE

FOUNDATION

Got Habits?
Creating Your Life Plan, One Step at a Time

Paradigm Shift
How You See the World

GOT HABITS?

Creating Your Life Plan, One Step at a Time

Hi… this is Glenn and I wrote this book. It is jam-packed with a bunch of good stuff about habits for people with disabilities. Oh wait. Did I just hear someone ask, "What's a habit?"

A habit is something you do over and over again until it becomes a part of who you are. When someone gives you a present and you say, "Thank you," this is a habit. People can have good habits or, sadly enough, bad habits. Same with people who have disabilities. A whole bunch of good habits can create a really good person. And I think you know what happens if a person chooses to have a lot of really bad habits.

Habits are like one big treasure map leading to your final destination. When you follow the map, you will arrive at your destination: a highly effective person with disabilities. While we have our own unique set of challenges, we also want to live the best, happiest life possible. This book will take you there!

I have always loved to draw. In fact, when I was in first grade, I won a school-district art competition. The reason I like to draw is because you can take a blank piece of paper, choose the tools you want to use (paint brush, pencil, crayon, etc.), and create a picture you enjoy. This is like the 7 Habits®. Together, we are going to take the 7 Habits and work our way through to being a kinder, more understanding, happier, stronger person.

This book is divided up into two parts: the Private Victory and the Public Victory. The Private Victory has three habits that will help us improve how we feel about ourselves and how we think about the world around us. The Public Victory will help us improve our relationships with other people. The last habit, Sharpen the Saw, is to make sure we are kind to ourselves and focus on continually keeping all of our newly learned habits.

Each new habit will be represented by one big "dot" on your treasure map, like this:

The Private Victory

The first three habits represent the Private Victory, which is all about you.

Dot 1.   Habit 1: Be Proactive—take charge of your thoughts and reactions.

Dot 2.   Habit 2: Begin With the End in Mind—start with a plan to get where you want to go.

Dot 3.   Habit 3: Put First Things First—decide what's most important.

The Public Victory

Habits 4, 5, and 6 represent the Public Victory, which is all about your relationships with others.

Dot 4.   Habit 4: Think Win-Win—find a way that works well for both of us.

Dot 5.   Habit 5: Seek First to Understand, Then to Be Understood— listening is more important than talking.

Dot 6.   Habit 6: Synergize—working together is better than working alone.

Renewal

Habit 7 is about taking care of yourself and ensuring you have balance.

Dot 7.   Habit 7: Sharpen the Saw—take care of your whole self.

As I present each dot, or habit, I'll introduce you to people with disabilities (PWDs). These people have chosen to create their very own treasure maps that have led them to be the best they can be. This helps them focus on what they can do (their abilities) rather than what they can't do.

Abilities for a person with DIS-abilities, you ask? Yes! Believe it or not, people with disabilities have countless abilities (what they can do) and not just disabilities (what they cannot do). I always say I've never met anyone who actually has a disability; they just lack some abilities. No matter how large or small your abilities are, you can learn to focus on what you can do and make this the biggest part of your day so you can live the fullest life possible!

Along with each dot (habit) on your treasure map, I will show you ways to put these habits into practice. Just like with everything else in life, the more you work on reaching each point on your map, the more likely you will be to reach your destination. By reading the words in this book and putting them into practice, you will learn to make the most of all your abilities, including mental, emotional, physical, and social. These abilities will help you to love your life more and more each day!

Got Habits?

When it comes to habits, I have found these quotes helpful, so I wanted to share them with you. Feel free to let me know what you think:

"Your beliefs become your thoughts,
Your thoughts become your words,
Your words become your actions,
Your actions become your habits,
Your habits become your values,
Your values become your destiny."

—*Mahatma Gandhi*
Former leader of India's independence

And this one:

"Nothing is stronger than a habit."

—*Ovid*
Roman poet who was eventually banished from society in 8 A.D.

Sadly enough, there's also this ancient proverb:

Bad habits are like a comfortable bed:
easy to get into but hard to get out of.

—*Anonymous*

Habits are what you choose to do over and over again to make your life better. But bad habits can work in reverse: if you pick up bad habits, your life will probably be more miserable. See what I mean?

To show what I mean, I have created the following 7 Habits of Highly IN-effective People With Disabilities:

HABIT 1: Don't be proactive. Don't take charge of your thoughts or actions. Just sit in a dark room, be depressed, and blame everything on your disability. Focus on what you can't do. Be a victim and figure this whole thing is totally out of your control and you can't do a thing to change it.

HABIT 2: Begin with no end in mind. Do not have any goals. Do not ever try to lead a better life. Let other people decide what your future will be. "You need to follow my plan," they will say. "If you do, then you will be happy, because I know what is best for you." Let others decide who you really are. To learn how to change this, see Habit 2: Begin With the End in Mind.

HABIT 3: Hmm, put important things dead last because what can you do? What do you have to offer? Put everything that doesn't matter first, like watching TV, playing video games, and being depressed. Do not worry about relationships and building them up; just put them on the back burner, because people should take care of you. Do not work on being a good child, sibling, neighbor, friend, or helping others. And why should you? You're the one who's got the disability. Everyone else should be building you up. Shouldn't everyone be helping YOU, O disabled one? To learn how to change this, see Habit 3: Put First Things First.

HABIT 4: Do not think win-win, think lose-win. Lose-win is like, "I lose and you win because I am a person with disabilities." Or, "My way will never be as good as your way because I am less of a person than you." And even, "My opinions don't count." Or you may even think lose-lose: "If I'm unhappy, then I'm gonna make everybody else around me even more unhappy." You can even think win-lose, so that you win but hurt other people—like thinking, "Don't help other people, because they should help you." That's the easy thing for you, but that can hurt a friend in need! To learn how to change this, see Habit 4: Think Win-Win.

HABIT 5: Get other people to understand you, don't worry about ever understanding them. "Because I have a disability, I don't need to listen to you. You need to listen to me. I don't need to understand you. You need to understand me." Sometimes a person with a disability will think, "My situation is always worse than yours, so you need to understand me first." Or some people with disabilities will think,

"You will never understand me and I will never understand you, so why try?" To learn how to change this, see Habit 5: Seek First to Understand, then to Be Understood.

HABIT 6: Do not even think about synergizing or working together with other people. When it comes to having some disabilities, my effort plus your effort doesn't equal much anyway. Therefore, I cannot cooperate with you, and I don't want to. To learn how to change this, see Habit 6: Synergize.

HABIT 7: Do not sharpen the saw, give up! Throw in the towel. Don't work on getting a better life for yourself. Do not try to improve your mind. Do not try to get physically stronger. Do not try to build warm and loving relationships. What's the use? Quit. To learn how to change this, see Habit 7: Sharpen the Saw.

So let's get started and, can I just say, you're not gonna believe how much the people in this book will help you. They say it takes a village to raise a child. I say it also takes a village to support a person with disabilities (PWD). I've had a great village to help bring out the best in me. I hope you find, within the village of this book, a lot of great ideas to help you live the best life possible!

SUPER ME

Suppose you were a superhero. What would you look like? What would your powers be? Okay, stop pretending. Make it happen!

Original painting by Glenn Stucki and Bart Hawkins.

PARADIGM SHIFT

How You See the World

For years I have had this dream to set my people free... my people with disabilities, that is. Martin Luther King Jr. has always been my hero because of a dream he had that all people should be treated equally. I also believe this is how people should be treated, but I think PWDs are overlooked when it comes to this.

Let me show you what I mean.

In 1993, I was in the fifth grade, and I had everything going for me. Yeah, I was only 11 years old and my life journey already seemed like one big Disneyland. This thought became my paradigm—the way I saw the world around me based on my center.

Let me break this down into bite-size pieces for you.

Each of us sees the world differently (paradigms). How we see the world is based on what we have decided is most important to us (our center).

In the fifth grade, I had this paradigm (view of the world around me) that my life was nearly perfect. My dad was a successful dentist, my awesome mom was a devoted stay-at-home mother, and I was the second of six children. Our family was living in Whittier, California. I was smart and popular, and people would smile at me and say, "He's gonna be a doctor someday." Other people would comment, "He is on track to succeed."

At this time, my paradigm was based on what people had told me should be most important in my life. Things like popularity and money. These things became my center.

"Your center?" you ask.

Yes. Our center is a place inside of us that represents what we stand for. This is a "values" place. It's where we go to make important decisions; like if someone asks you, "Hey, do you wanna go see this really gruesome movie?" you might ask yourself, "Is this what's important to me?" Maybe one of your values is to think good thoughts, and this movie might not produce good thoughts, so you'd say, "No, I don't want to go to that movie." The place you went to—mentally, intellectually, and emotionally—to make this decision is called your center.

A Paradigm Shift happens when we learn something new and see the world in a whole new way. Like, did you know that years ago, people thought the world was flat, until they learned it was round? Yeah, and people also thought the earth was the center of the universe until they learned the earth revolved around the sun. Funny, huh?

In this case, the paradigm was the way people saw the world (flat), and the Paradigm Shift happened when new information was received that helped help them see the world differently (round). I hope this book helps you have your own Paradigm Shift so you, too, can see the world in the best way possible.

Back to the fifth grade. At that time, like I said, my center was focused mostly on popularity, money, and what people thought of me. Within this self-centered world of mine, my parents were raising me on the 7 Habits, even though they didn't know it. They were proactive in choosing what success meant for our family and always had the end in mind. ("Glenn, clean your room or you'll be grounded!" Just kidding.) First things always came first, especially in our family, and they definitely had a win-win attitude, because our whole family loved helping people live better lives and having lots of parties where everyone had fun. Personally, I probably didn't seek to understand before I was understood at that time, but what kid does? I was definitely a team player (Synergize), though—not just on the ball field, but at school and around the neighborhood. And sharpening the saw? Our family was the king of constantly looking for ways to stay motivated and improve our lives through a weekly family meeting.

Sadly enough, I can honestly say that because of the person I was, had I seen a person with disabilities at this time, I would not have spent time trying to understand him or her.

Like I said, I was going places. My paradigm was set, and I loved it. My treasure map was taking me right to the world of lots of friends, big and important jobs, and lots and lots of money.

Then one day, I went on this jet-skiing trip with a bunch of people— me, my dad, and some other guys and their dads. We were going to Lake Mead, which is just outside of Las Vegas. We were all so excited. I had jet-skied before, so I was pretty good at it; but, at age 11, I was pretty carefree. I knew how to have fun, but I didn't think about a very important thing called safety.

About a year before we went on this trip, I saw an instructional video that showed two guys jet-skiing. It was so awesome. These guys were going really fast on their jet skis and were zig-zagging, making all these awesome patterns with their wakes, and I thought that was the coolest thing I had ever seen.

So when we were at Lake Mead, some of the dads were on the shore while some of the dads were in boats. And us kids? We were driving the jet skis all around the lake because we could at that time.

I was on a stand-up jet ski, all alone. I saw my two friends on a jet ski in front of me. I thought it would be so cool to cross in front of them, like I had seen in that video, so I did. Before I knew it, they ran over me. I flew off my jet ski like a rag doll and landed in the water.

People had to tell me what happened next because I was totally unconscious once I was in the lake. One of the kids jumped in the water and held my head up, so I wouldn't drown. One of the dads raced over in his boat to see if we were okay, but we weren't. They pulled me into the boat, and someone called my dad. I was in bad shape. After we arrived at the dock, an ambulance arrived and drove me to a Las Vegas hospital trauma center.

I was in a coma for about six weeks. While in this coma, I was in this dreamlike state, living my normal life like every other 11-year-old kid. I don't know how long these dreams lasted or how often they happened; but one time, while I was in this dream state, I went up to my room and I lay on my bed and had this, like, *Flight of the Navigator* dream. All of a sudden, my eyes popped open, and I was in this totally white room, and I couldn't move anything. Not an eyebrow. Not a toe. Not a pinky. And I couldn't talk, either. I didn't even know where I was.

Nurses rushed over to my bed and were doing stuff to me while I looked up at them and thought, "What happened? Who are all these people, and why are they here?" And then I saw my parents. I couldn't talk to them, and they were crying, and I couldn't figure out why. Was this for real? The only way I could cope was to think this had to be a bad dream.

I tried and tried, but I couldn't get any part of my body to move.

The Awakening

As I look back at this experience, I shiver to think how big this change was for me to go through. It was like someone had taken all the good dots (habits, accomplishments, everything) of my life up to that point and erased them from my treasure map. All I had now was an empty page. The beginning of my life journey was gone.

This definitely caused a Paradigm Shift. I mean, what could top this? Most people have Paradigm Shifts. They see their life one way, then they see their life another way; but this was my whole life changed in a flash! Even worse, it was forced on me. My center of popularity vanished. I couldn't laugh, cry, run around with my friends, or draw my favorite pictures. You name it, I couldn't do it. For the next minutes, hours, and days—I don't even know how long—I spent all of my waking time trying to figure out if this was a dream or something. How come I can't talk? Why can't I move? Slowly, people started explaining to me what happened and, even more slowly, I began to understand.

As I continued to come out of my coma, I could see something really bad had happened. I could also see that I could not do one thing for myself.

One thing that's also really important with *The 7 Habits of Highly Effective People* is the See-Do-Get Model. "See" is how you view the world around you (your paradigm). "Do" is the actions you take based upon what you see (your behavior). "Get" is what you receive as an outcome of your actions (your result).

Lying in that hospital bed was the perfect example of See-Do-Get, because all I could do was "see" my new world and wonder what I would be able to "do" (or in this case, not do). And I couldn't imagine what I was going to "get" as a result. Because of this, I was forced to see the world through what I call a new set of lenses. Sometimes we look at our world through a pair of very dark sunglasses, until we exchange them for a lighter pair. This is what is called a Paradigm Shift, only I feared I was changing my awesome pair of light-colored glasses for this awful pair of dark ones.

In many ways, I feel like I've lived two lives: the one before my accident, and the one after—like Christopher Reeves. He was a famous Hollywood actor who was also forced to have a Paradigm Shift. After playing the part of Superman in the movies, he took a terrible fall off a horse and became paralyzed from the neck down. Think about it. He once played the role of a man who saved people all over the world; and then, in an instant, he could hardly do anything for himself. The good news is, because he chose to focus on what he could do rather than on what he couldn't do, he became a real-life superhero as he chose to become the spokesperson for people with spinal cord injuries.

Or Stephen Hawking. He was like the smartest guy in the world! On his website, www.hawking.org.uk/, it says: "Stephen was diagnosed with ALS, a form of Motor Neurone Disease, shortly after his 21st birthday. In spite of being wheelchair-bound and dependent on a computerized voice system for communication, Stephen Hawking continued to combine family life (he has three children and three grandchildren) with his research into theoretical physics, in addition to an extensive programme of travel and public lectures... He always hoped to make it into space one day."

The guy had so much going against him, but he created so much more going for him. Stephen Hawking was unstoppable!

According to dictionary.com, disable is "to make unable or unfit; weaken or destroy the capability of; incapacitate."

Wow. This is the world's definition of a person with disabilities? I'm glad this isn't mine!

Paradigm Shift

The World English Dictionary isn't much better when it comes to helping us understand what a disabled person is. Its definition: "ineffective, unfit, or incapable, as by crippling."

Talk about a bad set of dots on a treasure map. This sounds like the definition of a person who is supposed to curl up in a corner and never say or do anything of worth ever again. I don't think so!

The following quote means a lot to me, but it means even more when you discover who wrote it:

> "When one door of happiness closes, another opens;
> but often we look so long at the closed door
> that we do not see the one which has been opened for us."
> —*Helen Keller*

Yeah, Helen Keller. Can you believe that? Helen got sick when she was only 19 months old and spent the rest of her life both deaf and blind. And she's talking about opportunities? This is because Helen Keller had a Paradigm Shift when she met Anne Sullivan. Helen was very angry and caused a lot of problems in her relationships with people. Anne came along and, because of her patience and knowledge, taught Helen how to read braille and communicate using sign language. Anne also taught Helen how to be a better person. This opened up a whole new world for Helen.

Hughes Martin is a friend of mine who made a huge Paradigm Shift. By the time Hughes was 42 years old, he had run dozens of 5Ks and 10Ks. He went on to run marathons, then he advanced to running four 100-mile ultramarathons! That's crazy! However, at age 44, Hughes was diagnosed with multiple sclerosis. He's now in a wheelchair with pretty much no use of his legs, but you'd never know it because Hughes always has a big smile on his face. Why? Because, as Hughes always says, "I accomplished more, for myself, in my 42 years than most people accomplish in their whole life, so I'm fine. I still like making the most of each day, just like I did before. Only now, instead of helping myself, I love making other people feel good. I do this by just being happy and showing them that no matter what happens to you in your life, you can still feel good about yourself and help other people."

Now's the time to create your own treasure map and work on your dots to create your very own life picture. What changes do you want to make when it comes to viewing the world around you? Do you complain a lot? Would you like to be more grateful? Maybe you spend more time thinking about what you can't do rather than what you can do. We all feel this way at times, which is why there are books like this one to give just the right kind of pick-me-up you need.

Baby Steps

One of the best ways to start a new habit is to take "baby steps." Babies crawl, then stand, then take their first step. You, too, can take your first steps:

- Make a list of some of the Paradigm Shifts you might have made in your life already. What did you do to make those shifts happen? Did you take time to listen and understand? Did you try something different and it worked? Like, maybe you were always bored on Sundays, until you started playing games with your family, then you ended up liking Sundays. That's awesome, so write this down, and don't forget it.

- Draw a picture of what your world once looked like through dark sunglasses, then what your world now looks like through lighter lenses. Make sure to include how you feel. I once drew a picture of my life before my accident, then in the hospital, then all of the things I've learned to do since.

- Talk to your friends and family about some of the great ways they see the world around them in spite of their obstacles. I have one friend who keeps a list of all of the things she can do. She adds to this list almost every single day.

- Talk to your friends and family about your greatest talents and how you could use them to help see yourself and the world around you in a better way. Maybe they have noticed that when someone is mean to you, you always smile back. Write down what your friends and family say, so you can go back and read these words on a day when you might need some encouragement.

- Read a book or search the internet to find out how people with disabilities learned to see themselves and the world in the best way possible. There are countless examples of people who succeeded in spite of their disabilities. This includes everyday people and people who are famous. Tom Cruise has dyslexia, which is a reading disorder; and Stevie Wonder is sight-impaired.

- Watch an inspiring movie like *Aladdin* or any other movie where the main character has superpowers. I love these movies most because they remind me of my own superpowers.

- Listen to happy, motivating music like "Hakuna Matata" from *The Lion King*, "Don't Stop Believing" by Journey, or one of your favorite tunes that helps you think about how good life really is.

You might not be able to change your disability, but you can change how you view your challenge(s).

Senior Steps

Because of her age, 90-year-old Afton shuffled with a walker and was always in quite a bit of pain. After looking at all the people with disabilities in her assisted-living community, she said: "I finally get it. Sometimes the only choice we have in this life is whether or not to be happy, no matter what happens." From that day on, no matter how much her health and strength continued to decline, she found something to be happy about. Because of this, she lived a better life for herself and for those around her.

YOU ARE THE CHANGE

I was inspired to paint this because Martin Luther King Jr. is my hero. He showed me how to stand up for what is right and make a change for love.

Original painting by Glenn Stucki.

PART TWO

THE PRIVATE VICTORY®

Habit 1:
Be Proactive®

Habit 2:
Begin With the End in Mind®

Habit 3:
Put First Things First®

HABIT 1

Be Proactive®

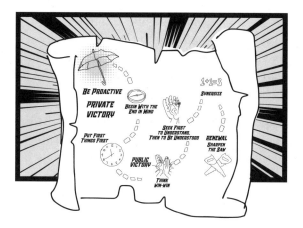

The first dot (habit) on your 7 Habits treasure map is: Be Proactive—take charge of your thoughts and reactions.

When I was in the hospital, my parents decided to transfer me to St. Jude's Rehabilitation Center in Fullerton, California, to be closer to our home.

As I continued to lie in that hospital bed, the only thing I had going for me was my thoughts. In my own effort to change my situation, I thought and thought about trying to move anything I could, but this was impossible. Then one day a saying came into my mind. It was something my awesome mom used to say to me (really, she is the best!): "Attitude is everything." So I thought some more and decided to try to move just one corner of my mouth. "I can do this," I thought. "I can." I pictured my smile and focused on the corners of my mouth over and over again for I can't even tell you how long. Then, BAM! Finally, one day, I did it!

My thoughts changed everything! Instead of lying in that bed, thinking my life was over, I chose to think about what I might be able to do. I'm sure my mouth moved the least amount anyone's mouth has ever moved before, but for a person who hadn't been able to move anything (and thought I might never be able to move anything again), this was the most amazing feeling I had ever experienced. It was all because I had decided to Be Proactive and think a certain thought. This tiny movement felt better than when I was elected president of my school.

But what I didn't expect was that, just because I had moved one corner of my mouth, everyone hugged me and patted me on the head and cheered and even cried.

Just because of one small, conscious thought ("I can do this!"), my whole world changed. At this point, my new journey had begun. Bring out the treasure map and add a dot, thank you!

Part of being proactive is understanding what you can change. One of the best tools for being proactive is to know your Circle of Influence® (the things you have influence over, like thinking good thoughts or helping other people) and your Circle of Concern® (the things that might affect you but that you have no influence over, like global warming or the national debt).

Sometimes Stephen R. Covey uses big words to describe easy ideas, like having a Circle of Influence and a Circle of Concern. Let me explain this a little more clearly so that we can reach a better understanding. I relate things to stuff I did as a kid. Like when I used to blow bubbles. The more air, or effort, I put into blowing my bubble, the bigger my bubble became, and it only grew bigger because of my effort.

As I lay in that hospital bed, I took one positive thought and all the strength I had, and put it into an area I thought I could most influence: my mouth. And my effort paid off. I had no idea how much this would affect my world, but it did. There was a lot I couldn't do (Circle of Concern), but smiling—the one thing I could do—had now opened my world up in a whole new way.

Visitors seemed to come more frequently. Therapists began working with me and people started to have bigger goals for me. You should have seen the uproar I created when my finger twitched. One… two… three times. That was another great puff of air into my big bubble! I focused on what I could influence, and it changed the attitudes of everyone around me. And I just kept on blowing, and expanding my influence, every single day.

We affect how big our bubble gets by trying new things, having a positive attitude, being friendly to others, or maybe making new friends by inviting someone we haven't met over to play with us. Our bubble shrinks when we are negative, argue, have a bad attitude, are mean to others, or don't want to communicate with anyone. It's amazing! All we have to do is blow into our bubble and as it grows bigger, we become happier!

Talk about influence. For the next couple of days in the hospital, more and more visitors came to see me. When they did, they said, "Look at Glenn. He's smiling!" as if they wondered why I would do this so much and not do something else, like move my little finger. That's because they didn't realize this was all I could do. But the more I did this, the more everyone started working with me. Suddenly, the doctors had bigger goals for me, and people started talking about the fact that, maybe someday, I might even be able to walk.

Accept What You Cannot Change, Run With What You Can

For people with disabilities, it can seem like we have very few abilities left, and accepting this can be very hard. For me, at this time, instead of focusing on what I couldn't do (my Circle of Concern), all I wanted to do was focus on what I could do (my Circle of Influence) to get back some control over my life. Just as Christopher Reeve chose to focus on the abilities he had left, now I had to focus on what I had left. Because of this, my smile became my superpower, and I wanted it to be the best smile anyone had ever seen before.

Recently, I received a letter from one of the kids on the jet ski that hit me. He said he remembered coming over to the hospital to see me. The minute he saw my smile, he knew I was going to be okay.

I'm not gonna kid you. The hardest thing I've ever done in my life was choose to "Be Proactive" in my nearly complete paralysis. But I had to, because that was all I had left. Choosing good thoughts was all I could do.

This is a stimulus-response situation. A stimulus is something that causes us to react (respond), like when we hear a loud sound and the loud sound causes us to jump. For me, lying in my hospital bed was a stimulus, and choosing what to do next was a response. The stimulus is the action; the response is the reaction. Between the stimulus and the response there is actually a pause, like when you're watching a movie on TV and you push the "pause" button so you can go grab a drink. In stimulus-response, this pause is what allows you to choose how you are going to react. Lying in my hospital bed after waking up from my coma, I used my pause to make the choice that I could smile. I did everything I could to smile, and it worked.

All of us experience stimuli every day: waking up in the morning, trying to find your shoes, being made fun of, etc. Just remember to pause and choose how you are going to react. If you can't find your shoes, pause or take a deep breath. I promise, you'll have a better response.

For those people who pause but choose not to take control of their life, the days can be very hard.

My mom told me that when I was just coming out of my coma, she said to my aunt, "Glenn is never going to go outside and play anymore, because I'm going to make sure he never gets hurt again. He is just going to sit on the couch for the rest of his life."

A couple of days after my mom said this, a lady was in the trauma-center waiting room while her daughter received lifesaving services. My mom and aunt started visiting with this lady and found out her three-year-old daughter had been sitting on the top of their living room couch, then leaned back and fell through the second-story window. The girl survived, but that was the last time my mother ever thought about having me stay home on a couch for the rest of my life because there was no guarantee I wouldn't get hurt there, either. Talk about a Paradigm Shift!

Now is the time to get off your couch, get moving, and take control of your life. You can do it! Just choose to Be Proactive. Focus on your Circle of Influence (what you can do) and not on your Circle of Concern (what you can't do). I'm not just saying this for you, but for me too. When people continually try to focus on my disabilities rather than my abilities, I sometimes respond to that stimulus by falling back into a state of helplessness. This can be discouraging, but just remember to pause and take charge of yourself by believing you can be the best you can be.

Thomas Alva Edison, also known as the Father of Invention, created over a thousand products. He also had a learning disability. His teachers thought his brain was "scrambled," but he never gave up. One of his mottos was: "If we all did the things we are capable of doing, we would literally astound ourselves." Now that's a guy who had to keep pausing and deciding that, no matter what, he was going to keep going!

Remember when we talked about the Paradigm Shift, or the new set of glasses ,we put on to see our life in a better way? A Paradigm Shift asks you to see the world in a whole new way. The dots (habits) on the page show you how to get there.

To create your first dot, Be Proactive, these baby steps can help. Possibly, you could do one or all of the following:

- Number from 1 to 5 on a piece of paper. Then write down five of your best abilities (what you can do). For example, you listen really well, you do what you are told, and/or you are kind and helpful.

- Ask other people what your abilities are, and add these to your list.

- Make a collage by gathering a piece of paper, some magazines, and glue. Cut out pictures of your abilities and glue them to the paper.

- Be more grateful and/or thankful by looking at all of the good things in your life and writing these things down so you won't forget them. If I told you to go out and find as many red Volkswagen cars as you can today, you would probably find 10 of them because you are looking for them. When we look for something, we usually find it. So look for things to be grateful for and remember these things over and over again.

- When a negative thought comes into your mind, pause and change it to a positive one. For example, if you think "I can't do anything," make a list of all of the things you can do. Maybe you remember to say nice things to other people or you always remember to say please and thank you.

- Compliment other people by saying things like, "You are a really nice person," "You have pretty eyes," or "I like your smile."

- Listen to a song that inspires you to be your best, like "You've Got a Friend in Me" from *Toy Story*.

- Get more enjoyment out of life by keeping a list in your mind of your close friends and good memories, like "My oldest brother helped me with my homework and this felt really good."

- Get the knowledge that you still have purpose by remembering you are loved by a lot of people, like your parents, grandparents, brothers, and sisters. My youngest brother, Jordan, always calls to see how I am doing, which is awesome and shows me how much I am loved. See how long you can make your list.

- Get the truth that you are a very important part of people's lives by remembering the compliments people give you, like "Glenn, your smile always makes me feel so good!"

Remember, you have so much to offer—even if it's only a smile. A smile is a huge thing! A smile can change the world, and that's awesome! Also, keep telling yourself that if you keep trying to do your best, one day, you'll be your best!

Now, onward to the second dot on your treasure map.

CHANGE FROM WITHIN

Butterflies inspire us to change for the better and see ourselves for what we can be.

Original painting by Glenn Stucki and Bart Hawkins.

HABIT 2

Begin With the End in Mind®

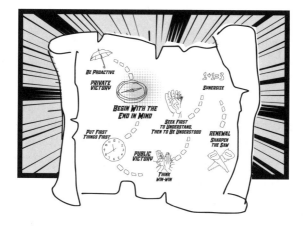

Our second dot, and another part of the Private Victory, is Habit 2: Begin With the End in Mind. This will give you the focus you need to get where you want to go.

Have you ever seen a horse run in a race? Sometimes horses wear what are called blinders. These blinders help them stay focused on seeing straight ahead instead of looking from side to side. Begin With the End in Mind also helps us see straight ahead instead of looking from side to side.

By now, you're probably thinking, "Are you kidding me, Glenn? I'm usually playing catch-up from behind rather than looking forward down the road."

Maybe this will help:

I have a friend who grew up across the street from Dr. William C. Tanner, who had a business called Thought Dynamics. Dr. William Tanner and his wife had 13 children. Every one of these children became very successful in pretty much everything they did. Most, if not all, of their children were straight-A students and leaders in their schools—either as the president of the school or as a cheerleader or something else that took a lot of work and dedication. These same kids went on to become college graduates and they were highly successful in each of their professions. Why? Because the dad taught his kids a really cool principle. He would tell them all the time, "However you picture yourself is usually who you are." This means that if we see ourselves as straight-A students, then we will want to do what it takes to become one. If we see ourselves happy, we will do whatever it takes to be happy because we began by seeing the end result of who we want to become.

He also believed this same principle has a lot to do with many of the tasks we do in this life. If you picture yourself liking a clean room, then you will have the motivation to clean it. If you picture yourself enjoying the rewards of doing well on your math test, then you will be more motivated to do the homework it takes to get a good grade. This is beginning with the end in mind.

TV commercials do this all the time. They show the end at the beginning. They show a happy person driving a new, shiny red car along the coast or a beautiful mountain road. This is because the car dealerships hope the people watching this commercial will think, "Hey, I can be that person too!" Then those people will start believing in this end in mind and, hopefully, do whatever it takes to buy that car.

So back to my hospital room. I'm in my hospital bed. I've smiled, and that was awesome. But like one dot leading to another, something else had to happen, because this was not going to be my end in mind. My end in mind was that I wanted to get out of that bed.

Even though this was true, there were times when lying in that hospital bed seemed like forever. Sleep and wake up and sleep again. And then I started to think, "Come on!"

Then one day I thought, "If this is a dream (because, literally, this was the only way I could cope with this traumatic change), anything can happen, right?" So I pictured myself getting up and walking over to the nurse's station, waving to everyone, and saying, "Hey, guys, it's me, Glenn. I'm okay now, so I'm just going to go home, okay?" In my mind, I walked by them and left the baffled nurses behind. I pictured myself turning around and saying, "You thought I had a horrible accident, didn't you? But I was just joking." This is pretty funny to think about now, because that picture I created was actually an end in mind. I had something to work for.

After days of lying in that bed and dreaming of somehow leaving that place, I started working even harder to… just… roll… over… and… BAM! One day I totally rolled onto the floor.

As I lay on the floor, buzzers went off and nurses came running in. They all looked at me like somehow the wind had just pushed me off that bed.

"Glenn, what happened? How'd you get down there?" said one nurse.

"Yeah... that's... amazing... really," said another.

"Ha!" I thought to myself. The doctors had told my parents I would be able to do hardly anything. But I knew right then and there I WAS going to get out of that bed and that hospital. I'd started working toward my end in mind.

From that moment on, I tried my hardest every single day to move something. Anything. And the harder I tried, the bigger and better the responses came—from me, my body, and all of those who continued to help me. Eventually, I was able to move my fingers, toes, arms, and legs.

End Result

Martin Luther King Jr. had a dream, and I had a dream. My dream was just beginning. I had one dot on my treasure map, and I could now see the second dot. Man, you talk about baby steps. In some ways, these were the smallest steps (not walking steps, but action steps) a person could ever take. But actually, these were the biggest steps I had ever taken. I had gone from doing nothing to doing something! This was the beginning of reaching my end in mind. Now all I had to do was figure out what other abilities I had, so I could figure out how to make a whole new life for myself. I knew I would never be "normal" again, but I also knew I was going to work hard to form a "new normal" that I would be happy with.

An artist goes to a beautiful place like a beach. He sets up his easel, places his canvas, takes his brushes, and begins to paint. He keeps looking at the ocean and then back at his canvas as he paints some more. Glancing back and forth between the ocean and the painting, he eventually completes his picture. The ocean represents our end in mind, and the painting represents our efforts to get there.

So, what is your end in mind? And how can you get there?

One way is to make your very own personal mission statement. A personal mission statement is kind of like a declaration. This statement defines who you want to be, how you want to live your life, and the things you want to do. Making a personal mission statement can sometimes take a while. When I created my personal mission statement, I first started with a list of my strengths and abilities. Once I realized what I was able to do now, I could decide what I wanted to do in the future.

As you will see throughout the rest of this book, my smile became my greatest ability. When I worked on creating my mission statement a few years ago, I wrote down, "Smile," then next to it I wrote, "Seeing my smile in my condition may help others smile in theirs."

This was a nice statement that defined how I wanted to live my life.

I then made a collage of pictures cut from the pages of a magazine. When I was finished, I looked at all the pictures and noticed that every one of them had to do with love. I already knew I wanted to help make a difference in people's lives because I'd thought about what I wanted to do with my ability to smile. So I put my smile and the love I wanted to share together to come up with my actual and literal personal mission statement: "Change the world with love." This has been, and will always be, the statement I hope people will remember me for.

About two years ago, while working as a cart pusher for Walmart, I thought about my mission statement and asked myself, "How can I change the world with love?"

I looked at all the customers and noticed the place where everyone parked the carts. It was totally empty and customers were standing there as if saying, "What the freak? This is Walmart. I need a cart!"

I thought, "I am going to make sure every customer has a cart. This is how I can begin to change the world with love." So I ran over and found a cart for this lady. Then I pushed another cart over to this guy and another guy, and I ran around speedy-quick. I got all of these carts for all of these people. Each one of them smiled and thanked me, and I knew I had started to change the world with love.

As we use our abilities to focus on our Circle of Influence, it grows bigger. Remember the bubbles from "Habit 1"? This happened for me because I knew my end in mind (to change the world with love). So I made choices that would make it happen.

Another time, when I was assigned to be a greeter at Walmart, I noticed all of these ladies with their kids and their sacks of groceries, and wondered how I could help them. So I asked if I could help load their groceries into their cars, and even made faces at the kids to make them laugh. I asked one of the moms how her day was going. When I was through, she said, "Thank you so much. You really helped me out a lot," and I knew I had made her day better. I kept doing this. Pretty soon, many of the customers became some of my best friends—like Jana.

Jana would come to Walmart pushing her son, Garren, who had cerebral palsy and couldn't talk or move anything. I would be so nice to her. I would exclaim, "Jana! How are you doing?" I would look at Garren and be so excited. "I love you, Garren! You are so amazing!" And I would give him a big hug. And then one day Garren got sick. Jana invited me over to their house to brighten Garren's day. I walked into his room. Tears streamed down his face as he recognized who I was. He got sicker and sicker until, one day, he passed away. The family asked me to speak at his funeral. I was so blown away. Because I had decided to change the world with love and make someone's day brighter with my smile, I was able to help Garren and even more people. Some people even came up to me after the funeral and said, "I wanted you to keep going because you were so inspiring." See how having an end in mind changes everything?

A friend of mine, Derek, is now 28 years old. But when he was 2 months old, he suffered a traumatic brain injury from a car accident. For most of his life, he suffered through frequent partial complex seizures. When he was 15, he had surgery and the doctors placed an implant in his brain that controlled his seizures. He still has some limitations, particularly a slight slur in his speech that others might feel shows some lack of intelligence, but don't kid yourself. Derek is very smart. As a young kid, Derek learned that nothing was going to get in the way of what he wanted to do.

Derek told me, "I learned to stay active as a kid." As he rested his white cowboy hat lightly on his head, I noticed his eyes matched the light blue in his plaid shirt. He flashed me another big smile. "Yeah, I always loved the adrenaline rush that came when I rode my bike over some pretty high hills with my brother." He laughed as if he'd gotten away with something people thought he might never be able to do.

"My motto is," he continued, "you can't live life accepting limitations. If someone tells you that you can't do something or are incapable of doing something, go ahead and do it, because if you don't, you might as well sit at home and do nothing all day. I know what my limitations are, but only enough to figure out what my abilities are. I love the feeling of adrenaline, which is why I love breaking horses." Yes, this is what Derek does. He breaks, or trains, horses. Physically, this is not an easy task, but it doesn't stop Derek.

Another friend of mine whom I love is Marlow. Marlow has Down syndrome. He also works at a movie theater. He says his mission statement is, "I stand for my family. I can take care of my family by helping. I can make dinner. We can play games together or we can watch a movie. I support my brother and sisters."

Some people create their mission statement, or their end in mind, by writing their epitaph. "What's an epitaph?" you ask. An epitaph is a one-sentence statement people who have passed away have engraved on their headstone to define the life they've lived. I remember reading one guy's headstone that read, "Grumpy." This is definitely not the end result I am working toward.

Joseph is my best friend. He has Down syndrome. He used to work at a grocery store with me. He loves watching John Wayne movies to relax. His mission statement is: "You are my friend." To him, the whole world is filled with friends.

A few years ago, Stetson, another friend of mine, was in a farming accident that left him with some physical disabilities. His mission statement is: "Be a positive influence and be happy."

Amber is a girl whose brother was in my grade. She and her brother are twins. She has some facial deformities. She says, "I love to read books and be with my family while doing the things I love. I love to serve others because I enjoy seeing smiles on other people's faces. I like going on walks with my dog. It brings me so much joy because she is my baby." Her mission statement is: "Happiness comes from accepting the bodies we have been given as a gift and enhancing our natural attributes, not from remaking our bodies."

Remember how I said that before my jet ski accident, everyone thought I was going to be a doctor? Well, after my accident, I knew this was never going to happen. But that was okay. When I made my mission statement, I realized that, in some ways, being a doctor and being a greeter at Walmart both have the same end result. Both professions influence lives for good. After all I had been through, I had been given this chance. Isn't that what life is all about? Because of this, I came to the conclusion that my past was over and done with. I could only change the present and the future, because those were what I had influence over.

Let's get out our treasure map. We have now arrived at Begin With the End in Mind, where there are several baby steps you can take:

- Create a phrase or statement that defines who you are. Write it down. Laminate it. Read it every day. Share it with others.

- Select one word that describes how you hope people will remember you—for example: "happy," or "giving," or "kind."

- Draw a picture of the person you want to be. Hang this on your wall to remind you.

- Make a collage that shows the kind of person you want to be and hang this somewhere where you can see it.

- Pick a song or write a song or poem that inspires you to be your best.

A famous author, Napoleon Hill, had a disabled son who was deaf as a result of being born without ears. My favorite quote by Napoleon is "A goal is a dream with a deadline." This is what we're talking about: dreams that lead to goals that then become habits.

And speaking of habits, let's move on to our next one.

OUT OF THIS WORLD

I painted this for a cashier's son at Walmart. He asked me how much he should pay for it, and I said a hug would be payment enough.

Original painting by Glenn Stucki.

HABIT 3

Put First Things First®

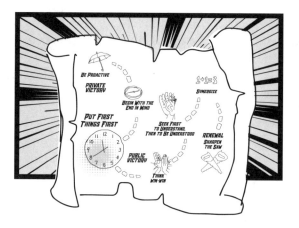

Facing Real Life

In the Private Victory of personal growth, the next dot on your treasure map is Habit 3: Put First Things First.

Going back to my accident and recovery, after months of working in a rehabilitation center, I was finally able to discover more of my abilities, like talking and walking. Finally, I was able to go home, where I was homeschooled.

As I got stronger and stronger, I quickly learned that people had other ends in mind for the new, disabled me. But they wouldn't tell me what those ends in mind were. Instead, they would tell someone else, like my parents. Because I was now a person with disabilities, everyone thought I couldn't understand as I much as I did. Like the time my team of doctors told my parents, "We have great news! Because Glenn is doing so well, we think he will one day be able to get around in a wheelchair and maybe even take special-ed classes where he might be able to learn a few skills here and there. Isn't that wonderful?"

My parents were like, "Are you kidding?" They knew I was once a smart kid, and they believed I could do much better than what was being presented to them. So they Put First Things First and searched around until they found a school in Utah that would let me attend regular classes while taking special-education classes to catch up.

Because of what they felt was most important—to see that they and each of their children lived the best life possible—they moved our family to Utah where I could attend a local middle school.

When I started school, I remember thinking, "Everything is so hard now." Even though I was more independent, parts of my brain still didn't work, so everything felt a billion times harder. "Aargh!" I would scream at times. "Everything used to be so easy!"

I would limp down the halls at my junior high school trying my hardest to get to class on time.

Because of my obvious struggle, classmates would yell, "Hey, Gimp!" and "Yo, Freak!"

I would look around and see everyone's eyes staring at me—following me all the way down the hall.

"Why are you all staring at me?" I would think. "I AM NORMAL! I want to be just like you, SO QUIT STARING AT ME!"

Then there was the time I was in my high school's common area having a good time with my friends (meaning I was just standing there, listening to them talk back and forth), when someone flicked a penny at me.

"Ow!" I yelled, rubbing my forehead. "That hurt! Why are you doing that to me? Do you think I am stupid or that I don't know what you're doing?"

I didn't want to be the freak everyone thought I was. I looked around and caught sight of the most popular kid in school. I knew he was the one who had done this to me. All I could do was think about how I just wanted him to be my friend.

I had a lot of other tricky things happening as well. People would say to me, "Go over there, Glenn, and sit down. Don't talk. We need to take care of you now." These comments seemed like a way for people to tell me my life was over. And I thought it was just beginning. I felt like people were saying I needed to be boxed up and shipped away to a safe place where I would never get hurt again.

That was great for them. However, if this were the case, I would never experience the best of what life had to offer. There would be no more bad days in my life, but there would be no more good ones either. If this were the case, then what did I have to live for? What good would all of these newly learned abilities do for me if they didn't come together and create the picture I wanted?

If I had listened to all of this advice and not known what was most important to me, my life would have been sooooo pointless. But I couldn't listen. I didn't want to. Why? Because these people didn't know me. They didn't know what I had been through and survived. Even though I had physical changes and limitations, no one seemed to understand that I still felt like the same Glenn I had always been. But to everyone else around me, it was as if the old Glenn had died and the new Glenn was incapable of doing anything. When would everyone realize I was just as normal on the inside as I was on the outside? When was everyone going to look at me for my abilities and not my disabilities?

Because of these thoughts, I had to figure out what was most important to me or I would have gone crazy. I had to decide what would be first in my life. I had to find what I could depend on. My inner belief system came first, then my family. They had saved me. After this, my smile came next, because my smile had saved me too, and it was going to help me stay connected with other people as well.

These things were the center that kept me going when I was yelled at or made fun of. First and foremost, these beliefs were what formed my center from which everything else flowed.

"Men are not prisoners of fate, but only prisoners of their own minds," said Franklin D. Roosevelt, the thirty-second President of the United States, who became paralyzed and ended up in a wheelchair as a result of having polio.

Making a Difference Through Time Management

Even though no one else seemed to believe in the new me, I did, and that made all the difference. I wanted to "change the world with love," and I put this first in my life because nothing else really mattered. I definitely was moving forward on my very own treasure map.

Oftentimes people think PWDs do not need to have priorities or put First Things First because PWDs have enough to deal with just living life with less. However, not having priorities creates its own disability. If you do not create first-place dreams in your life, you will end up living with second-place rewards.

Amazingly enough, I actually had so much going for me that I had to start managing my life by organizing my time so I could end up exactly where I wanted to be and create my own first place. Now that I was out in the real world, I tried to do something—anything—to have a plan. But I wasn't very good at it.

At that time, I didn't know about the 7 Habits Time Matrix® plan. I was pretty much working with my own time-management program called SMWGNF, or Spinning My Wheels Going Nowhere Fast.

Check this out. This would have helped me so much and can really help you. I'll show you what I mean:

Quadrant 1: "Urgent and Important" is for things like:

- Medical emergencies

- Taking prescribed medications

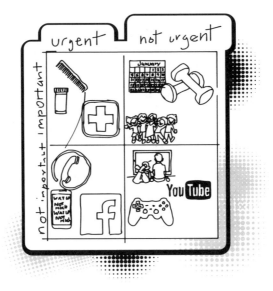

You do not want to miss any of the items in this quadrant. They are all both urgent and important.

Quadrant 3: "Urgent but Not Important," sadly enough, is where we usually end up spending most of our time, because these things feel urgent. But they are not important. Things like:

- Facebook

- Texting

- Talking on the phone

Quadrant 4: "Not Urgent and Not Important" is just time wasted. Even though we sometimes use this quadrant to relieve stress, we shouldn't spend too much time here. Things like:

- Watching endless television

- Playing video games for hours

- Watching YouTube videos

Quadrant 2: "Not Urgent but Important" is actually the most important overall. This is where most of our time should be spent in order to accomplish the goals we want. Things like:

- Planning our time wisely

- Working out

- Spending time with friends and family

- Doing things that help us reach our end in mind

It's not that we should spend all of our time in Quadrant 2, but we should spend most of our time there. Stephen R. Covey once said, "Most of us spend too much time on what is urgent and not enough time on what is important." My mission statement, for example, of changing the world with love isn't urgent; nothing terrible will happen if I don't take steps toward that goal. But it is important. And doing things every day that contribute to that end in mind are the most important things I can do. I have to put those first things first.

A good example of putting first things first is Heather Whitestone. When Heather was born, she had problems with her ears and could hardly hear. Because of this, her doctors believed she would never get past the third grade. They must have been surprised when she went on to become the first woman with disabilities to become Miss America. This was in 1995. Heather accomplished all of this because she prioritized what was most important in her life and then made goals to accomplish her dreams. After becoming Miss America, she went on to graduate from college and write three books. I'm sure Heather spent most of her time accomplishing her goals as she would have listed them in Quadrant 2.

Then there was Tom Dempsey. Even though he was born without toes on his right foot and no fingers on his right hand, he became a kicker for the New Orleans Saints. He even kicked a 63-yard field goal that broke the NFL record by seven yards. He, too, had to prioritize his time in order to practice and practice and practice until he eventually became one of the best kickers in the world. Being an NFL-level kicker isn't exactly urgent—if Tom Dempsey hadn't made this kick, the world would have kept going—however, because this was important to Tom Dempsey's end in mind, he had to create a Quadrant 2 priority to make it happen.

I may never kick a ball as far as Dempsey, and that's okay. My record-breaking moments come in making other people's lives better by trying to make changes for the better in my own small way. Unlike my old approach where Quadrants 1, 3, and 4 were most important, I had to change and focus on the items found in Quadrant 2. And this is where people with disabilities can excel. If the people in my community would just harness their abilities, manage their time, and help other people with disabilities learn to be leaders, maybe we'd be recognized instead of overlooked.

If you are going to have priorities, then you must decide what they are. Stephen R. Covey said relationships are the most important. I may have trouble with numbers or running in a race, but I can do something about the relationships in my life by planning for them and carrying out my plan as I would outline in Quadrant 2. It's easy and doesn't take a lot of effort. You can even plan to do things like more small acts of kindness. Make it a priority, write it down, and make sure that happens before anything else.

For me, there's a natural high that comes from serving other people. It is definitely better than sitting in a wheelchair or on a couch all day thinking about how your situation is worse than anyone else's. It sounds crazy, but you can change things; you can make your most important things happen by managing your time wisely. Decide what is most important, then prioritize. Put this in your planner or on your calendar. I'm not only talking to you, I'm talking to myself too. I've been in that wheelchair. I've sat on that couch. Doing things for other people creates new stories in your head for you to think about. Many times when you're just living life, wonderful stories come back to you—like the laughter I got from the kids when I made the funny faces at Walmart or speaking at Garren's funeral. That's why I make sure to set aside time for my relationships. For you, it will be setting aside time for what's important to you.

Looking how far you've come on your very own treasure map, "Put First Things First," here are a few baby steps you might want to try:

- Make your own Time Matrix (quadrants), using the drawing on page 58. In each square, write down how you spend your time. This helps to show how much time we waste. In Quadrant 2, list how you could spend your time better.

- Write down the names of the three most important people in your life. Under each name, list the reasons why each person is so important to you. What does each do that makes you like him or her so much? Like my mom. I like her because she helps me so much.

- Add your name to the top of this list, then write down ways you can develop the same traits as the three people you like most. Because of my mom, I want to be more helpful.

- List all the different roles you have in your life—brother or sister, friend, leader, or employee. How you could make these relationships stronger? Write these ideas down on a calendar so you can have a date to carry them out.

- Throughout each day, keep in mind what is most important to you. Write these ideas down. Post this on your wall or bulletin board so you can have more good ideas in your head than bad ones.

More of your time will be spent on more important things if you pay attention. Because of this, you will have more rewarding experiences.

BEST FRIENDS

The bond we form with our best friends is unlike any other. It brings us happiness and peace when we see them. That's why I have a lot of best friends.

Original painting by Glenn Stucki and Bart Hawkins.

PART THREE

THE PUBLIC VICTORY®

The Emotional Bank Account (EBA)

Habit 4:
Think Win-Win®

Habit 5:
Seek First to Understand, Then to Be Understood®

Habit 6:
Synergize®

THE EMOTIONAL BANK ACCOUNT [EBA]

We've talked about the first three of the 7 Habits on our treasure map: Be Proactive, Begin With the End in Mind, and Put First Things First. As was mentioned in the beginning of the book, these three habits are private habits. Because of this, they belong to the Private Victory. These internal goals strengthen how we feel about ourselves—something we refer to as our Emotional Bank Account.

We have now arrived at the Public Victory part of the book. These are the habits we need to help us in our relationships with other people. But before we move on to those habits, let's talk about having an Emotional Bank Account (EBA).

This bank account works a lot like normal bank accounts, with deposits and withdrawals, except this bank doesn't have any money in it. Instead, it collects the actions and words of the people around us. Deposits into an Emotional Bank Account are things like saying thank you, giving a hug, or doing something nice for another person. A withdrawal would be something like calling someone names, hitting somebody, or not keeping a promise.

When I was younger, my dad did a lot of things for me. He read me books at night (deposit) and listened to me when I was sad (deposit). Then every once in a while, maybe my dad would lose his cool with me (withdrawal) or accidentally run over my bike in the driveway (withdrawal). Remember that, Dad? Just kidding. Over the years, my dad and I have made enough deposits into each other's EBAs that a withdrawal, every now and then, won't hurt us. But let's say I have just met someone for the first time, and that person made fun of my disability. Now this is sensitive to me and, if I don't know this person, he or she has already started out with a withdrawal. Which means my bank account with this person is in the negative. But maybe we can start being nice to each other, so we can make deposits into each other's account to see if we can build a more positive relationship.

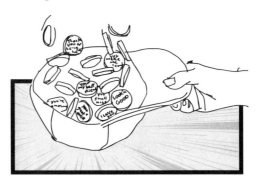

This reminds me of a trip my friends and I took to Neptune Park. This park is unlike any other park around, because it has this huge 30-foot-tall pyramid made of metal and netting. In fact, this pyramid is the tallest climbing pyramid in North America and is one of only three pyramids like it in the world.

Oh man! This pyramid looked like it would be so much fun to climb, so I started my way up. All of a sudden, I noticed this kid in my group looking at this big contraption with fear in his eyes. I took a step back and thought, "What can I do to make this kid happy (deposit)? Would helping him climb up this thing be the deposit he wants?" So I asked him what he would like to do.

"I want to play Pokémon," he said.

Really? I'm just about ready to climb one of the most awesome pyramids in the world, and this kid wants to play Pokémon? I had no idea how to play that game. I grew up not even liking it, mostly because I didn't understand how to play it. It was the last thing in the world I wanted to do, but I could tell that it was important to him.

So I asked, "How do you play?" And he started to explain to me, with all of this enthusiasm, all of the different Pokémons and the mutations they went through.

"Okay, let's play," I said, and climbed down the pyramid.

Now, I just gave this kid a huge deposit, because I was willing to do something he felt more comfortable doing.

If your Emotional Bank Account is full, it doesn't bother you when someone comes along and makes a withdrawal. Like, one day, I had a great morning with people doing and saying a lot of nice things. Then someone said something mean, and I was stopped by a policeman and had to take a breathalyzer test again, like I always do, because they think I'm drunk when it's really just the way I walk and talk. These were all withdrawals from my Emotional Bank

Account; those things have been withdrawals in my relationships with those specific people. However, if someone calls me stupid or says something else that's really mean, these things don't bother me. I have already decided that, no matter what, no one is ever going to rob my Emotional Bank Account of all the good deposits I've collected over the years. Ever. Because of our challenges, I think people either believe that PWDs automatically walk around with negative Emotional Bank Accounts and that there is no way out of this, or that we are just fine living with a lower quality of life. Some people also think people with disabilities can't ever feel good about themselves. They think, "How could they? They have a disability. They have deficits." What they don't realize is that we are no different inside from anyone else. We deserve healthy relationships, and our Emotional Bank Accounts can—and should—be full of really great deposits.

Your relationships with other people can be made stronger by doing things you promised to do or by doing small acts of kindness. I love doing small acts of kindness. My smallest act of kindness, that actually makes the biggest impact on people around me, is my smile.

Another way we can improve our relationships is by saying we're sorry when we've done something wrong. Saying you're sorry to another person is like what an eraser does to a chalkboard—it erases the mistake. We all do things wrong. Luckily, saying you're sorry helps make wrong things right again. And if, for some reason, the other person does not accept your apology, at least you have "owned" your mistake.

One thing you could do right now to build more bridges between you and other people is to pick one person you can build a stronger relationship with. Say something nice, or do something nice, or just say you're sorry if you've done something wrong. You'll be amazed at how easy it is to make any relationship stronger.

This part of your treasure map is so important. Here are some baby steps that will help you build your Emotional Bank Account and have more positive relationships with other people:

- When someone asks if you can help, practice saying yes as much as possible. These are opportunities to make deposits into other people's EBAs.

- If you see someone having a bad day, ask the person if there is anything you can do to help. This is also a good deposit into someone else's account.

- Surround yourself with people who build you up, and stay away from people who try to make withdrawals from your EBA.

- Make a list or collage of all the different ways you could help make other's people's lives better.

- For only one day, try to say something nice to everyone you see. You will be so surprised at how much this one act can really help brighten your day and theirs.

I love the EBA because making others feel better always makes my life so much better!

Now that we've talked about the Emotional Bank Account, let's look at the three habits that will really make sure our relationships with other people are the best they can be! Get ready to add one more dot, the fourth habit, on your treasure map!

KNIGHT

I painted this for a kid I swam with in the morning named Xander. Every time I asked him how he was, he would nod his head. When I asked him if he wanted a painting, all he said was, "I want a knight on a horse." It was up to me how to interpret the rest. He is my best friend now and talks to me when I ask how he is doing.

Original painting by Glenn Stucki and Bart Hawkins.

HABIT 4

Think Win-Win®

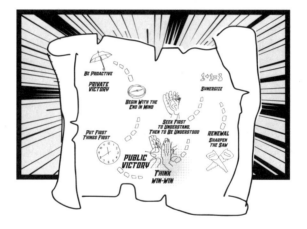

Think Win-Win, the first habit in the Public Victory, is so important in your relationships with other people. Man, I can't tell you how many times I have, as a person with disabilities, felt like I was in a lose-win relationship—like the time I got flicked in the forehead with that penny! Loser! At that time, I believed I was less of a person than those around me, so I felt I deserved what happened to me. I thought that whoever flicked that penny at me was cooler and better than me, and I must have done something that made me deserve that—even if it was just the way I looked or acted. Wrong!

There was also a time in my life when I would be with other kids who didn't have disabilities, and I would think, "Because you are higher-functioning than me, let's just go with what you have to say." Even if I knew I had a better idea, I went with theirs, because I thought I was the loser and they were the winners.

Win-lose is like being at the top of a totem pole with everyone else underneath you and thinking, "I can only win if you lose." In my special-education class, there were times I thought I was better than all of the other students around me because I was higher-functioning. This was the wrong way of thinking, and I understand it now.

And lose-lose is even worse. Lose-lose says, "If I'm going to lose, then you're going to lose too." We can even think, "Misery likes company." Or, "If I'm going to be miserable, then you are going to be even more miserable." With these types of thinking, we usually start losing our connection with people. Fortunately, I had a lot of support from those around me to help me see the best, rather than the worst, of what life had to offer.

You have to believe you are a winner to create a win-win situation; you have to proactively believe you deserve to win. For me, getting to a place of win-win was a process.

Let me give you an example. After I graduated from high school, I became pretty independent. I tried so hard to believe in myself and my abilities, and I finally decided to quit worrying about what I couldn't do or what everyone else thought about me. I decided to be happy, no matter what, and to even be funny—especially to be able to laugh at myself.

During this time, I was ready to move forward to higher and better places for me, so I said to everyone around me, "I want to go college." And you know what they said? I thought they would say, "That's terrific, Glenn. Look at how far you've come!" Instead, their reaction was, "No, Glenn. We don't think college is for you. We think maybe you should try to develop some type of trade." Trades, like plumbing or construction, can be good for some people; but I knew I could do more. For me, this felt like a lose-win situation—they were the winners and I was the loser.

I was like, "Are you kidding me?" After all I had been through and worked so hard to overcome, I felt like people were trying to erase the person I wanted to become. But I knew even better plans were in store for me. I may have suffered a traumatic brain injury, but a lot of my brain still worked. It was as if people had forgotten this fact!

So I thought to myself, "No, I don't think so!" I started writing off their loser plan for me, and I started creating my own end in mind. I called the local university and started taking classes. But still, my family and friends were writing off my goals and plans. They'd smile and pat me on the back and say stuff that sounded like, "You keep going to class, Glenn, and when we decide what you can really do, we'll let you know." Again, lose-win.

It may have taken me longer than most, and I may have had to repeat many classes. Finally, with the help of all of the people who did believe in me (and spoke to me in win-win ways), I was able to walk across the university stage and receive my bachelor's degree in behavioral science. All of my friends and family were so excited, which I looked at as a win-win situation.

Then everyone said, "Now what?"

What happened next changed my life forever.

Transition Person

Remember how I mentioned that when I was in first grade, I had won a school-district art contest and always loved to draw? Seeing how I had done so well in one area of school, I decided to try another. Knowing how much I loved art, I decided to take an art class.

So I took this one class and started creating all of this art by haphazardly painting rapid, wide strokes back and forth across the canvas. I thought this type of painting looked really cool. This is how I knew to paint my best and, until I was taught differently, this is how I was going to continue. My teacher looked at my work and said, "This is amazing, Glenn!" Each piece I created, no matter how good or how bad it was, she would announce, "Another masterpiece! A real masterpiece!" She did this over and over again, until I started to wonder if she was really sincere. One day, after showing her my latest creation, I said with great confidence, "Do you know how long it took me to paint this one?"

She said, "How long?"

MY SMILE IS MY SUPERPOWER

I spread my arms wide and declared, "Only one half hour!" She smiled and waved her arms wildly at my creation and announced, "It's an accidental masterpiece!"

Then she looked at me and said, "And you are a savant!"—meaning an idiot savant.

I was like, "Huh?" I had no idea what a savant was until months later when I was taking private lessons from that same art teacher's aide, Luke. Luke had pulled me aside during one of those "masterpiece" classes, and said, "Would you be interested in taking classes privately? You really do have talent."

While taking his class one day, he told me what an idiot savant was. Luke's definition was like the one I found on Merriam-Webster.com. It says an idiot savant is "a person affected with a mental disability (as autism or mental retardation) who exhibits exceptional skill or brilliance in some limited field (as mathematics or music)—called also savant."

"What?" I thought. I lacked normal intelligence but had unusual mental abilities? Was I being labeled again? I had abilities! I had a bachelor's degree! When would people see this?"

I was stunned. I couldn't believe this. It was as if my art teacher thought I was the accidental masterpiece. But Luke helped me improve my talent by taking time with me and believing in my abilities. Luke took care of my style and taught me the things I could add to make my talents stronger until my art projects became real masterpieces and not just accidental ones.

"I took Glenn under my wing," says Luke. "Glenn was one of my first private students. I had to teach him how to focus and not give up on himself. For me, I have anger issues because of my minor scoliosis and my inner-ear imbalance. Because I get frustrated sometimes, I can sympathize with people with disabilities. Art helps me calm down, focus on the moment, and actually concentrate on the tip of the brush. Art slows your heart rate. Glenn has had to learn to do this. I have had to teach him, and he has done real well."

Luke was what the 7 Habits refer to as a Transition Person. Stephen R. Covey said, "A Transition Person is one who breaks the flow of bad—the negative traditions or harmful practices that get passed from generation to generation or from situation to situation, whether in a family, a workplace, a community, or wherever." Luke helped me break my flow of bad thinking.

It's like the song, "If you see a frowny face, change it to a smile." This is a transitional song and pretty much describes what a Transition Person does. He or she helps you turn your frowny face into a smile by being there for you—not as a judge, but as a light. They are healers and not victims, and they help you believe in yourself and become a better person. Luke knew I had potential, and he stuck with me until I became the artist he knew I could and wanted to become. He didn't think of me as a person with disabilities; he saw me as an artist. This was a win-win situation. Luke was, and still is, a definite gem on my treasure map.

Other people's reality for you may be that you are disabled, but what is your reality for yourself? You still have many abilities and ways you can make a contribution to others; and they, in turn, will be grateful. This is also a win-win situation.

For me, win-win means helping other people feel good. When we make them feel good, we end up feeling even better. And sometimes all it takes is a smile. Win-win feeds off of itself. Relationships change the world. How do you want to change the world? With love? gratitude? kindness? acceptance? Or something else? That's where the Circle of Influence and end in mind come in—what can I change, what do I want to change, and how can I change it? As I work on my ability to change the world with love, maybe I can change someone else's world. And if I could influence someone— like the next Martin Luther King Jr.—that could change the world! That would be a win for me and a win for the world.

Win-win includes cooperation—working together to figure something out. Win-win says, "Let's figure this out together so that we can we both come out ahead." If you value your relationships, you are not going to want any of them to lose. Win-win is what helped me come out of my dream and start making decisions about my reality.

Many times I thought back to that situation where the kid hit me with the penny. How I could have made that situation turn into a win-win? I could have said, "Ow," and then looked down at the penny and added, "Oh look, someone just lost their penny." I could have picked it up and handed it to the person and said, "Did you know that as long as you have a penny, you will never be penniless?" And, hopefully, that would have made them all laugh, and I would have appeared to be friendlier.

In special ed, instead of thinking I was so much better than all those people, I could have dropped those barriers and said, "How can I help you?" Or, "This is how you can do that better." It would have helped the other kids—and it would have helped me change the world with love.

Win-win is one of life's biggest treasures, and following baby steps can really help make all of your relationships more positive. Try one of these:

- Without caring who wins or loses, play a game with another person just for the fun of it. Maybe don't even keep score and make it a game where everyone wins.

- Look for opportunities to compliment those around you, and do it. Watch what happens. The better you make others feel, the better you feel. This is win-win at its best!

- Do you have a problem with another person right now? How could you cooperate with that person to turn this negative situation into a win-win? Put this in Quadrant 2 and on your calendar, and start working on it now.

- Choose a person and make a plan to be a Transition Person for them by being less judgmental and more peaceful. Help the other person believe in himself or herself by listening and supporting them. Stick with them until they succeed. As a result, you will feel your own success.

- Do small acts of kindness. My younger brother Jake took the time to help me learn how to use my air brush, and this meant the world to me. It helped me a lot with my art, but it also helped him feel good.

The more you practice the habit of win-win, the more positive relationships you will have and the happier you will be. Take time to look around you. Is someone else feeling left out? Ask them what's wrong, or start playing with them. Always treat everyone equally.

Go ahead. Start now, and enjoy the results today!

This is what Martin Luther King Jr. was talking about when he said he had a dream that one day all people would be treated equally. We want that too, right? Then let's look at the next dot to see how we can achieve this.

SOMETHING GREATER

This represents us looking at our potential and thinking, "Can I do this?" As a member of the disabled community, I am often thinking this same question. The fact is, with enough will and imagination, anything is possible.

Original painting by Glenn Stucki and Bart Hawkins.

HABIT 5

Seek First to Understand, Then to Be Understood®

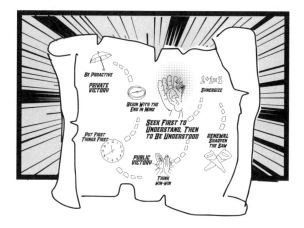

The fifth habit on your treasure map, and the second one to fall under the Public Victory, has to do with understanding. A Roman philosopher, Lucius Annaeus Seneca, once said, "One of the most beautiful qualities of true friendship is to understand and to be understood."

Think about it. The more you understand someone, the more likely you are to have a better relationship. You have to understand them first. Then, and only then, can you help them understand you.

Let's says you want to bake a cake. First, you need to understand how to bake a cake by following the directions. You need to know all the ingredients. Then, you need to know how much you need of each ingredient. Next, you need to know what type of pan you should bake the cake in. Then, you need to know how hot the oven should be. Finally, you need to know how long the cake should be baked. Wow, that's a lot of understanding before you even start making the cake. But this is important, or you will not have a good cake!

Just like it takes a whole bunch of understanding to create a delicious cake (yum, yum), it also takes a ton of understanding to create successful relationships.

Let me show you what I mean. One time I saw this man resting against the back side of a couch in a lobby. He held himself up with two crutches, both his feet were wrapped with loose bandages, he had a scruffy beard, was wearing a baseball cap, and kind of looked like an ex-con. My friend went up and started talking to this guy. Later, I asked my friend who the guy was, thinking this guy might have been someone who shouldn't have been hanging around this nice lobby.

"Oh, that guy?" my friend said. "That's my dad. I don't know if you know, but my dad has cancer, so he's not feeling so great."

Oh man. I felt about 1 inch tall. I made a judgment before I took the time to understand or ask questions. I, a person with disabilities, was caught in the middle of a quick reaction and was way off on my assessment. I'd judged this guy without knowing all his parts, just like so many other people have judged me. I apologized to my friend and then felt even worse when he said, "It's okay, it happens all the time."

I learned that day that the more we seek to understand, the truer our view will be. Let's say I ask you to draw me a tree. In order to draw the right tree, you'll need to understand a few things first, like what kind of tree? A palm tree? A Christmas tree? An oak tree? How tall should this tree be? How long do you have to draw this tree?

Remember the time I went to the park and tried to climb that pyramid? That poor kid was too scared to climb the pyramid, and I asked him what he wanted to do. What he needed was important to me. When I took the time to understand what he wanted, that made him feel understood. But before I played Pokémon with that kid, I had to get down from the pyramid. While I was climbing down, I started to get dizzy. I looked at him standing there and knew I had to help him understand I was in trouble. So I said, "I'm disabled; I need help." This kid was probably 10 years old, but he said, "Put your foot right there. Now here. Back up there. Oh wait, now here. Okay, slow down." He even helped make my shaky legs stop shaking. He was willing to take the time to understand my needs and help me because I took the time to understand him and Pokémon and what would be best for him. And when he did, I was ready to listen and learn all I could from him. Our understanding worked in a circle, and it made a huge difference. Seeking first to understand actually worked to my benefit!

When it comes to understanding others, we need to ask more questions and ask the right questions. This helps us see the whole picture rather than just a piece of it. When we seek to understand others, what we're really doing is showing respect for another person by choosing to see things as they really are and not just guessing.

We also need to remember to ask appropriate questions. I remember one time I was at the community pool that I go to every morning to swim laps. I have to wear this ankle brace on my foot to keep my foot from "dropping." Sometimes I'm afraid people are going to laugh at me or think it's gross or just too weird.

While putting on my brace in the locker room, Dave, one of my best friends, asked, "What are you putting on?"

Instead of being disgusted and saying something mean, he asked me an appropriate question. So I explained to him how the brace worked.

"Cool," he said. And he even helped me put the brace on—all because he took the time to understand.

And then I asked him a question. "Dave, what do you do to get better at swimming?"

"I just keep practicing."

Look at the people around you, especially the ones who say all the wrong things or sometimes say mean things. Ask yourself, "Why would a really smart person say something so hurtful?" Maybe they had a bad day? Maybe they don't understand, and you can help them.

I had a friend whose brother died of AIDS. A lot of people said some really rude things to her. One girl even said, "I bet you're glad your brother's dead."

WOW! That's horrible! She didn't even take the time to understand that my friend loved her brother and was sad when he died.

This friend told me that she cried to her sister about this, and her sister said, "We belong to a very elite group of people now. We belong to the club of those who 'get it' when it comes to losing someone from AIDS."

PWDs belong to their own club of those who "get it." People without disabilities sometimes say inappropriate things because they've never taken the time to understand the pain and suffering (or the joy and rewards) that we go through. They have no idea how it feels.

It's not very often that you'll see a PWD speak harshly to another PWD. We know what it feels like to deal with the issues that come with our set of challenges. And I'll tell you one thing, I'd rather be a member of the "I get it" club than a member of the "I don't get it" club or even the "I don't want to get it" club. So in this way, people who seek to understand before they seek to be understood are very fortunate.

Once, I had the chance to be the one asking the right questions. It happened when I was swimming at the local recreation center (the same place where I wore my ankle brace). When I first started swimming laps there, there was this man who always swam in the lane next to me. The swim team swam in all of the other lanes, but the public had to share two lanes. This man was the dad of one of the swim-team members, and he used to pull on my fins. I thought it was because it bugged him that I was there swimming in the public lanes. So one day I asked the swim teacher, "What's the deal with this guy?"

"I'm not sure, but I know he used to be on his college's swim team. And so maybe he thinks he should get more of the pool than he does, so when people get in his way, he does stuff like pull on their fins."

Instead of reacting to him in a mean way, I took time to ask the swim teacher why the man did this and took the teacher's thoughts into consideration. Once I understood he wasn't after me personally, rather than yelling at him or telling him to stay out of my way or telling him, "Hey, look mister. I have a disability. You get out of my way. You need to understand me. I'm the one with the disability. You need to yield to me," instead, I took the time to understand. And if I helped him, maybe someday he'd help me.

"Maybe I'll just stay out of his way more," I thought. By trying to understand his perspective, I changed my paradigm. He was just trying to swim really fast and I was getting in his way. By acting in a way that wouldn't annoy him, I was able to be seen as a person instead of something getting in the way of his workout. Eventually, he and his son started talking more kindly to me, and we got to know each other and ultimately became good friends... all because

I took the time to understand. Seek First to Understand, Then to Be Understood.

Sometimes PWDs think, "Because I'm the one with the disability, I don't need to understand you; you need to understand me." This statement actually promotes disability thinking because it says, "I don't care about you, but you have to care about me—no matter what." This is the opposite of seeking to understand. These statements say, "You need to understand me before I'll ever try to understand you." This does not work.

Another thing that helps is I'm not afraid of my disability. Whenever I introduce myself, I always tell people, right away and with great confidence, that I am disabled. This is so I can take the lead in helping them seek to understand me. I feel like I can talk to them better and understand them better. See how this works?

If you don't want to be seen as disabled, then try not to let your emotions control you. Try not to act emotionally disabled either. One of the ways this can be done is by listening to other people first. By learning about them, and even trying to walk in their shoes (or in my case, sandals, because I'm such a beach-going kind of guy), we get a chance to understand their perspective.

Here are a few baby steps to help you when it comes to arriving at Seek First to Understand, Then to Be Understood on your treasure map:

- Write down the names of three people you would like to understand more about. Make a plan to understand them more by listening, asking questions, and even try repeating back a few of the things you've heard so they'll know you really listened.

- Keep better eye contact with the people you talk to. This also shows them you are listening.

- Sometimes the best view of a forest is not when you are among the trees, but when you have taken a step back to take a look over the forest. Take a step back in your relationships and look for better ways to understand and serve your loved ones. Write these things down, and make a plan on how to carry it out.

- Next time you want to keep your feelings inside, share them in a nonjudgmental and an understanding way after you've given the other person a chance to explain his or her feelings.

- When listening to someone else, do not respond too quickly to what they're saying. Take a moment to think, then respond.

Understanding is a full-circle process. Like a boomerang: whatever understanding you give or "throw out there" will come back to you the same way. And that can be a win-win, can't it?

Now, we all know scissors are used to cut things, right? I am going to show you another thing about scissors that you probably never knew, but that will help you so much in your journey to live a fuller life.

DRAGON'S ROAR

I was inspired to paint this for my best friend Titus. I snuck up behind him holding the picture, and when he turned around, he was so surprised he started crying.

Original painting by Glenn Stucki.

HABIT 6

Synergize®

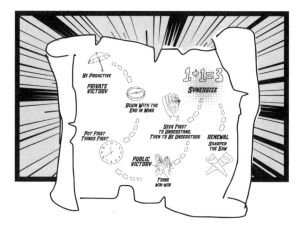

The sixth and last habit to fall under the Public Victory is Synergize. For most people, synergy is 1 + 1 = 3. This equation doesn't come as easily to people with disabilities, but it is possible! Anything is! Damian is my friend who has autism. In addition to autism, he has speech apraxia. This means there is a disconnect between what he thinks and understands, and what he is saying. Damian didn't start to speak when everyone else did. This caused a lot of frustration for him. The more he wanted to speak, the less he could. With Damien, something was missing, so he couldn't learn how to talk by observation. This is like 1 + 1 = 0, so his parents decided to try something different: sign language!

"We started using sign language with him. This lessened his frustrations. However, not everyone knew sign language. He still felt uncomfortable being around others, so he only stood next to those that he knew could understand him. His world was still small.

"When Damian was in third grade, he began to speak. As time went on, his vocabulary slowly grew and the less he used sign language. The more his vocabulary grew, the more his world opened up and he felt comfortable around more people. We were so excited for his determination and hard work. Every year, he adds more words and sounds to his current vocabulary.

"Now Damian is 16 years old and he has a broad vocabulary. He doesn't use sign language very often. Most kids at his age who have his disability have a vocabulary that won't continue to grow. However, Damian is different. He is continuing to learn new words and make new sounds. His drive to continue to grow is amazing."

This is 1 + 1 = 3.

Synergy is possible with us, it just may take effort in finding the right route. It's kind of like Christopher Columbus. Everyone thought he was crazy sailing out into the ocean. "He might fall off the edge of the world," they thought. He took his idea to the queen, who supported him, and he sailed off to find another route to India (or so he thought). Eventually, he found the right route to another land. This opened up the world to new ways of learning. The queen's support, plus his effort, opened up a whole new world, literally!

This is where the biggest part of my dream has been fulfilled. When I woke from my coma, I had to figure out how to cope with my new circumstance. I decided I was in a dream. Then I saw these pictures of superheroes that my uncle drew for me, and they sparked an idea that I was in a good dream. Anything could happen in a dream, and since I was in a good dream, I had an idea to smile. I like to think that my smile is synergistic. My smile helps other people. Synergy starts with a simple smile because this becomes a sign that "think cooperation" is an option. Doctors, nurses, therapists, visitors, friends, and family all synergized to keep me happy, and I had my pictures to look at to set my imagination free. I could begin to Synergize with them and begin to soar again. Synergy is possible no matter what stage of life you are in. The basic definition of synergy is one idea combined with another idea will lead to outcomes greater that what they should be.

The Wright Brothers are a huge example of two people who worked together to come up with an idea that would change the world. This is something they never could have done on their own. When Orville and Wilbur Wright were young, they loved things that could fly, including a helicopter-type machine that flew with the help of a rubber band. As they grew older, they started a business building bikes together, but they couldn't get the idea of making a flying machine out of their mind. First, they started building kites together, then they built gliders, and finally, they created an airplane that flew for twelve seconds. Can you imagine how fun that would have been? Eventually, they built an airplane that could fly across the ocean. That's amazing, and a huge example of what can happen when two people work together.

We cannot make it through this life without the help of others. Oftentimes, for a person in my community, this is even more true. Synergy means one plus one doesn't equal just two, but three or four or more. Let's say I don't have any legs and I am just on the floor... like a beggar. Did you know that the word "handicap" comes from the old English term "beggar," meaning a person with a cap in their hand, begging? We are not beggars, but people of great worth. We are only beggars of other people's understanding and acceptance.

Let's say there is a blind guy who also needs help getting around. My eyes can compensate for his lack of sight. His feet can compensate for my legs. He can help me walk. I can help him see. This is synergy. We value our differences and compensate for what we lack by using another person's strengths.

One great example of synergy is a pair of scissors. In order for the scissors to work, both blades are needed. On their own, the blades are incapable of doing anything, but together, they can cut paper and any number of other things.

Another comparison could be the Reese's Peanut Butter Cup. Chocolate, on its own, is amazing, right? And then you've got peanut butter. Wow! I mean, who doesn't like peanut butter? Both flavors sell millions of dollars on their own, but then someone had the idea to put the two flavors together and BAM! An even more popular flavor was invented, which is awesome. And can I just apologize to the peanut-allergy community for what I just said? 'Cause I have a cousin, Asher, who is seven years old and has a severe peanut allergy. It's so sad that even one small peanut can cause such a life-threatening situation. Yet, it's true, and my cousin is so amazing. He is not sad. He just walks around with his EpiPen, or shot, in his backpack, and he gets on with his life, thanks to an incredible support system filled with people who help him see the bigger picture.

In art, synergy is the point at which one color mixed with another color becomes even more beautiful, like blue and red mixed together make purple. Yellow and blue mixed together make green. Synergy is everywhere and is what makes a lot of things work better than they could alone.

Differences Are Good

Synergy is what makes all our differences make sense. Salt plus more and more salt will only make your turkey taste really, really salty. But salt with a little pepper can complement your meal nicely.

Every person on earth is here to offer his or her part in this life. If we were all the same, we would not be able to learn from each other, help each other, and serve each other. Our differences are what make life so wonderful and what makes it possible for us to get through this interesting journey together.

> "If you want to go fast, go alone.
> If you want to go far, go together."
>
> —*Old African proverb*

Remember when I was at the park climbing that big pyramid? I couldn't get down. I didn't know how I was going to do it. And then this kid said he would help me. I could have done it all by myself if I wanted to struggle, but it was much easier with his help. He helped me, and I helped him by giving him the opportunity to do something nice by talking to him and learning a little bit about him.

My art teacher Luke's abilities mixed with my abilities created a masterpiece. Helen Keller and Anne Sullivan are also another example of synergy. With Anne's help, Helen accomplished something she never would have been able to on her own.

Henry Ford, who created the automobile and also created one of the first health systems that treats PWDs, said, "Coming together is a beginning; keeping together is progress; working together is success."

Take the word *disability*. The word means "lacking ability." If someone lacks an ability, then someone else who has that ability can help them. This is synergy.

Before my accident, I looked at PWDs as if they were from another planet. I remember this one kid vividly. He had a black flattop, huge glasses, and eyes that were crossed. He talked with a slur and had two leg braces. When he walked, his arm came up, and I think he limped. I thought he was so different from me. I never would have imagined I would be in the same boat with him just a few years later.

If I would have just talked to him, I'm sure I would have noticed that he was no different from me. Maybe I could have noticed things he could do that I could not do. I can't walk normally. I can't talk normally. I can't even think normally at times. But when I'm thinking of how to help others, I quickly forget how different I am. This is also a form synergy.

Even after my accident, there were times when I looked at people with disabilities and dismissed their potential, until I realized this was because I didn't like myself. It wasn't until I met Jen that I began to understand that I wasn't alone when it came to feeling this way.

Jen was in a wheelchair and there was very little she could do. My uncle told her about me and how I had some challenges. Because of this, she didn't contact me for a while. Jen has her master's degree in math. She told me she thought it would take five minutes for me to move 5 feet, so she didn't call me for months. When I met her, I couldn't believe how smart she was. We would go out, and sometimes she would get food on her face, and I loved taking care of her, and then it hit me, "Is this what people feel like when they take care of me?" I loved being able to help someone. This is synergy. She did the logical thinking. I did the funny, creative thinking. Together, we clicked.

For your next dot, Synergize, the following baby steps will help you have stronger relationships:

- Make a list of five popular relationships (and other things) that are better together than apart—like Batman and Robin, *Apollo 13* and Mission Control, Prince William and Princess Kate. Write down what makes these partnerships work—like both partners are nice to each other, both partners share the same goals, etc. Then write down what they do together that they can't do apart.

- Write down some of the relationships you enjoy because of the synergy you feel: your parents, your best friend(s), your doctor, etc. List what skills you have that work well with each of these people and make the relationship better. For example, I always remember how my oldest sister, Sarah, took me over to her house and one of her kids said he was glad I came over so I could share my happiness.

- Write down one or two people you have a relationship with that might be weaker than you would like. Think of two strengths you have that could help complement the other person and help him or her believe in himself or herself. This is a win-win, because you make the other person feel good and you get to help someone out, which is awesome. Synergy is a natural overflow of win-win thinking.

The best part of synergy is all of the positive energy that comes with it. There is a high that comes from accomplishing so much more with another person than you would have accomplished on your own. This is the theory behind "the village." It takes a village, working together, to help raise a society to its highest level possible. You, too, can be part of the PWDs village.

Go ahead and put another dot on your treasure map. Now we're ready to place the very last dot and arrive at our destination. Soon you will become a Highly Effective Person With Disabilities! Awesome!

HORSES

I painted this for my best friend Robby. Before I painted it, he said he wanted to be my biggest donor. At the time, we had someone who donated 750 dollars for a painting. He said he would donate 1,000 dollars. All the while I was painting it, I was thinking, "Is this a thousand-dollar painting?" I kept painting and painting until, at last, I was satisfied.

Original painting by Glenn Stucki and Bart Hawkins.

PART FOUR

RENEWAL

Habit 7:
Sharpen the Saw®

The Final Masterpiece

HABIT 7

Sharpen the Saw®

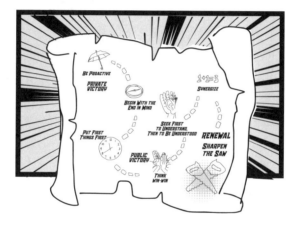

The last dot on your treasure map is Habit 7: Sharpen the Saw.

In his book *The 7 Habits of Highly Effective People*, Stephen R. Covey tells the story of a man sawing down a tree. The man had worked for so long to cut the tree down that his saw became dull. Because he didn't stop to sharpen his saw, he found that his saw became more and more dull. The man just kept using the saw, taking more and more time to cut down that tree. If only he had stopped to sharpen his saw, he would have cut the tree down a lot quicker and easier.

This is what Sharpen the Saw means. When it comes to our lives, we need to stop and sharpen our saw so we can do things quicker and make our lives easier.

Just like our job, where we work five days a week and then take two days off to renew ourselves, the 7 Habits work the same way. We have discussed in detail six great habits that WILL help you create one awesome life picture. The seventh habit is for the purpose of renewal—for making sure you keep yourself living at your strongest level possible.

When I was younger, my family would go to the park and sometimes—if we could talk them into it—my parents would push us on the merry-go-round. My brothers, sisters, and I would climb on and my parents would start to push us. This was hard at first, but as the merry-go-round went faster, the task of pushing it became easier. When the merry-go-round reached its desired speed, all our parents had to do was tap the merry-go-round to get it to maintain its speed.

This book has been about creating new and good habits. At first, creating a new habit is hard. But as we push ourselves and eventually get the forward motion going, all we have to do is tap, or renew, these habits to keep them moving forward.

When it comes to sharpening your saw, there are four different parts to renewing yourself.

Physical—taking care of your physical body with exercise, sleep, or eating healthy.

Social/Emotional—service, compassion, laughter, or good times with friends.

Mental—reading, writing, planning, doing puzzles, or painting.

Spiritual—meditating, studying fine art, listening to classical music, or experiencing nature.

Renew and Revitalize

People with disabilities have so many ways to renew themselves physically, mentally, spiritually, and emotionally.

Art is a customer who comes into the Walmart where I work. I noticed something different about him, so I said, "Hey, how are you? I'm Glenn, and the reason I limp is because I have a disability." And he said, "Oh, I have a disability too. I had a stroke." So we got to know each other and have been good friends for about five years. I asked him a couple of weeks ago what he does to renew himself, and he said, "I spend time with my grandkids." The stroke just happened a couple of years ago, but he's found ways around it so he can continue to live a full life.

Lauren is from Boston, Massachusetts. She has some learning disabilities. Lauren's way of renewing herself is through reading. She sharpens her saw socially because she loves making other people laugh and she loves to laugh also. Laughter will always be the best medicine.

In spite of my friend Dylan's TBI (Traumatic Brain Injury), he loves to accept challenges. And this goes along with his mission statement: "Challenges are a chance to better yourself." He loves to listen to music, play Minecraft, and take his dog on walks. He also loves to build things with his LEGOs because it is so good for his imagination.

Angela is a friend who lives in Boston. She has cerebral palsy and her way of sharpening her saw is to go on walks and work out at the gym.

Elizabeth has a fused left hip and deals with depression and anxiety. "What relaxes me," she says, "is serving others. I like to crochet and give my crochet projects to other people. My eight-year-old son is autistic, and his way of relaxing is to read and talk."

Megan is the daughter of an amazing anthropology teacher I had. She is fantastic! She has Down syndrome. Megan keeps her sense of humor every day. To keep her spirits up, she says things like, "Holy Moley Catcha Toley." Her favorite activity to sharpen her saw is going to the theater and watching plays like *Les Miserables*.

Greg is the best. Greg has Down syndrome. Greg likes to laugh and dance. Anything he finds funny, he repeats. His hugs are the best, and he hangs on to them. If he can't remember names, he calls people Moe. He always calls me Allen. But Greg renews himself by making other people happy.

I sharpen my saw intellectually by working at Walmart. Talk about fast thinking—nonstop. My brain is exhausted every day, but I'm getting used to it. And some of my efforts pay off socially, like this note I received the other day:

> Dear Glenn the Greeter,
>
> Hi this might be weird but oh well. I just wanted to write you a thank-you letter. Thank you for just... being you! You are phenomenal at your job. I've never really paid attention to the Walmart greeters, but I pay attention to you.
>
> I don't know how you feel about your job, but I am extremely grateful that you have it. Whenever I walk in and see you, it brightens up my whole day. I could be having the most terrible day ever, then I see you and it turns the whole day around. You're so energetic and you always have the hugest smile on your face.
>
> You've made an impact on my life. Thank you.
>
> Love Hannah

My saw is sharpened mentally by cashiering in the garden center at Walmart. One day, a mom and her son came through my line. They were smiling and talking happily. I thought, "They are my friends," so I told them I loved them. I overheard the mom say to her son as they walked away, "Isn't he a nice guy? We should all try being more like him." This made me feel really good.

But the best way I sharpen my saw is through my art, because it is both relaxing and challenging. It also builds me physically, mentally, spiritually, socially, and emotionally. It works my body. When I practice, the quality gets better, and I get faster. It works my brain by challenging my thinking and creativity. It works my soul because it helps me to be in touch with the wonders of the world. It works my heart because I don't paint anything for myself. It's all for other people. See what I mean by changing the world with love? First, I started giving my paintings away to everyone on my swim team. My first one was to a kid named Scott for his birthday. I painted a second one for him because I thought he liked the first one so much.

He looked all surprised and confused with my generosity and said, "But Glenn, it's not my birthday!"

So I said, "I know. I'm just giving you this painting because I love you."

When I give people one of my paintings, I tell them, "Don't tell anyone that I didn't sell this to you but gave it to you because I love you! Take this. I love you. I totally love you." This sharpens my saw.

On your treasure map, you can Sharpen the Saw by doing the following baby steps:

Body

- Start enjoying healthy foods.

- Develop a workout routine that actually relieves stress and makes you feel better.

- Sit outside and enjoy all of the sounds you hear.

Mind

- Listen to relaxing music or even stress-relieving sounds like ocean waves or raindrops, etc.

- Close your eyes and, starting at your toes, say, "My toes are so relaxed." Then focus on your legs and say, "My legs are so relaxed." Keep going through all of your limbs, your back, your neck, all the way up to the top of your head.

- Learn an inspiring poem or quote. Close your eyes and repeat this while feeling its calming effects.

Heart

- Tell people you love them.
- Laughter IS the best medicine. Take life more lightly, tell more jokes, watch funny movies, and find more ways to laugh every single day.
- Start thinking more with your heart than your mind.

Soul

- Meditate more often.
- Read inspiring words.
- Serve continually.

Other words to describe Sharpen the Saw are:

- Rejuvenate
- Renew
- Restore
- Recover
- Revitalize

It is so important to recharge your batteries and spend time sharpening your saw so you can continually have the energy and the desire to constantly improve your path. This is the best part of the 7 Habits—that we can relax and renew in order to always feel our best!

SMILES ARE CONTAGIOUS

Mascots are so inspiring to me. I have been able to work with the Mascot Miracles Foundation. They rally together with lots of mascots to help terminally ill children have good last days.

Original painting by Glenn Stucki and Bart Hawkins.

THE FINAL MASTERPIECE

Look at your map! Look what you've done! You have arrived at the best "you" that you can be! Do you not love this sooo much? I do!

Keep going, that's all. Don't quit. You were born for a reason: to make a contribution. By now, you should know what your contribution is. Congratulations!

Wow, here we are—at the final destination on our wonderful 7 Habits treasure map. Awesome! Don't you love it?

In the beginning, I had a dream. The only way I could cope with my circumstances was to think I was in a dream. My dream became a reality, but my dreams have never really ended and never will… because I dream of people with disabilities being recognized for what they can do.

My dream happened when I lay in that hospital bed and had to accept the fact that I had experienced a horrific accident and had new limitations in my life. I worked hard to push forward—and past a lot of disabilities—to see if I could walk and talk again. I am so fortunate that part of my efforts worked. Then I learned to incorporate the 7 Habits and I was able to take charge of my life: Begin With the End in Mind; Put First Things First; Think Win-Win; Seek First to Understand, Then to Be Understood; Synergize;

and Sharpen the Saw. These are the dots that completed my map. One by one, each of these habits can be learned and acted upon. If only more people with disabilities would learn how to use these abilities, they would not be so minimized or underused or frowned upon. Instead, they would flourish and grow and lead.

For a person with disabilities, the miracle of learning new habits is no different than the sun rising to give light or the rain falling to water our plants so they can produce fruit. These miracles happen quietly and one step at a time. The greatest miracles of all time are not reserved just for geniuses. Do what you do best, keep doing it, keep doing it, and keep doing it some more. Blow away all those art teachers; blow away all those people who want to flick pennies at you, until you reach your highest height. You can connect all the dots, create your life picture, and make all of your wildest dreams come true!

"All our dreams can come true—if we have the courage to pursue them," said Walt Disney. He had his own learning and life difficulties, yet he chose to focus on his abilities and went on to create "The Happiest Place on Earth," otherwise known as Disneyland.

You, too, can watch your dreams come true. If I can do this, you can too. Help the dream of people with disabilities being treated equally come true by starting today to create your very own dream—one habit at a time—until you find all of the gems needed to live the best life possible. You can do this. No matter what your disability is, you can: make a valuable contribution to those around you, feel purpose in everyday living, and enjoy the rewards that come from living a habit-centered life.

We all are Martin Luther King Jrs. in the making. We just need to learn to be proud of who we are and tap into all we really can do.

Congratulations. You did it! You can now be the best person you want to be, because you have all the gems you need from our fantastic 7 Habits treasure map! And remember always... Glenn Stucki loves you!

ABOUT GLENN

Born in Torrance, California, Glenn Stucki is the second of six children. He has devoted several years to helping "set his people free." Every morning, he can be found swimming lanes at the American Fork Fitness Center and then smiling and greeting each person who enters the local Walmart where he works as a greeter. When not busy with these tasks, he is immersed in creating his latest acrylics masterpiece or helping other people with disabilities find their abilities.

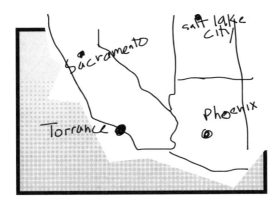

CHANGE 4 LOVE

Glenn cofounded a nonprofit called Change 4 Love. It helps people with disabilities discover what they can do to change the world. Change 4 Love also inspires kids with amazing artwork and support. Change 4 Love was founded by Glenn Stucki and Bart Hawkins. Bart has a degree in business and is highly proficient in art. He teaches art therapy to people with special needs. He and Glenn met in Glenn's short stint in UVU's art program. Glenn called Bart because he needed support if he was to make his goals a reality, and Bart was the perfect fit. Bart also has a degree in art management and a degree in art and visual communications. Their organization was founded in 2016 and has already inspired well over 50,000 kids in just two short years! Find out how they are changing the world one painting at a time and show your support by visiting them at www.Change4Love.org. They have a gift for everyone who supports them, so visit their page to find out more.